Mapping Global Issues

Rain Forest Destruction

Mapping Global Issues

Rain Forest Destruction

Peter and Antonia Littlewood

A⁺

Smart Apple Media

Published in the United States by Smart Apple Media
PO Box 3263, Mankato, Minnesota 56002
Copyright © 2012 Arcturus Publishing Limited

This book has been published in cooperation with Arcturus Publishing Limited.

Series concept: Alex Woolf
Editor and picture researcher: Alex Woolf
Designer: Jane Hawkins
Map illustrator: Stefan Chabluk

Library of Congress Cataloging-in-Publication Data
Littlewood, Peter.
Rain forest destruction / Peter and Antonia Littlewood.
p. cm.—(Mapping global issues)
Includes index.
 Summary: "Describes the causes of rain forest destruction and what the effects of fewer trees has on the environment and societies around the rain forest areas. Includes maps and charts"—Provided by publisher.
ISBN 978-1-59920-512-0 (library binding)
1. Rain forest ecology—Juvenile literature. 2. Rain forests—Juvenile literature. 3. Rain forest conservation—Juvenile literature. 4. Deforestation—Juvenile literature. I. Littlewood, Antonia. II. Title.
QH541.5.R27L49 2012
333.75'16--dc23
                                    2011017067

Picture credits
Corbis: 9 (Martin Harvey), 19 *bottom* (Karen Kasmauski), 21 (Collart Herve), 28 (Danny Lehman), 31 (Yusuf Ahmad/Reuters), 38 (Howard Davies), 43 (Ashley Cooper).
Getty Images: 41 (National Geographic).
Shutterstock: 14–15 (Frontpage), 19 *top* (Frontpage), 20 (Dr Morley Read), 24 (guentermanaus), 33 (Csaba Vanyi), 39 (Mike Price).

Cover picture: A selection of rain forest burns along route BR-364, the main road through Rodonia, Brazil.

Every attempt has been made to clear copyright. Should there be any inadvertent omission, please apply to the publisher for rectification.

Map sources
7: Various sources; 11: The Nature Conservancy; 13: WWF; 16: Brazilian Institute for Geography and Statistics, La Déforestation en Amazonie; 23: Electrobras; 27: World Resources Institute; 35: National Geographic Map Machine; 37: Global Forest Watch, Cavalli-Sforza, Luigi Luca.

Printed at CT, China
SL001637US

PO1040
08-2011

9 8 7 6 5 4 3 2 1

Contents

What Are Rain Forests?

Imagine yourself in a dense, green forest. It's midday, but there's lots of shade, provided by the huge trees that tower 200 feet (60 m) or more above you. Every now and then, you stumble on an exposed root. The sweat soaks through your shirt in the hot, damp atmosphere as your boots tramp through a carpet of leaves that cover the muddy ground. The air around you is filled with sounds—the buzzing of insects and the strange calls of birds and monkeys. Occasionally, a grunt from the undergrowth startles you as you walk through the rain forest.

Tropical Rain Forests

Most rain forests are located in the tropics, which are the warmest part of Earth. The tropics of Cancer and Capricorn are 23.5 degrees north and south of the equator. Tropical rain forests cover approximately 6 percent of the planet's surface. Before we started clearing the rain forests, they covered up to 14 percent. They experience annual rainfall ranging from 8 feet (2.5 m) to 33 feet (10 m).

Temperatures rarely fall below 68° F (20°C) and can exceed 86°F (30°C). Humidity in the rain forest can reach 100 percent. As the sun is almost directly overhead throughout the year, there are no distinct seasons. Tropical rain forests cover approximately 5.8 million square miles (15 million sq km) of the planet's land surface. Key rain forest zones are the Amazon rain forest in Central and South America, the Congo Basin of

FACTS and FIGURES

RAIN FOREST STATISTICS

- Every second, a slice of rain forest the size of a football field is mowed down. That's 86,400 football fields of rain forest per day—more than 31 million football fields of rain forest each year.

- Covering less than 2 percent of Earth's total surface area, the world's rain forests are home to 50 percent of Earth's plants and animals.

Source: The Nature Conservancy, www.nature.org

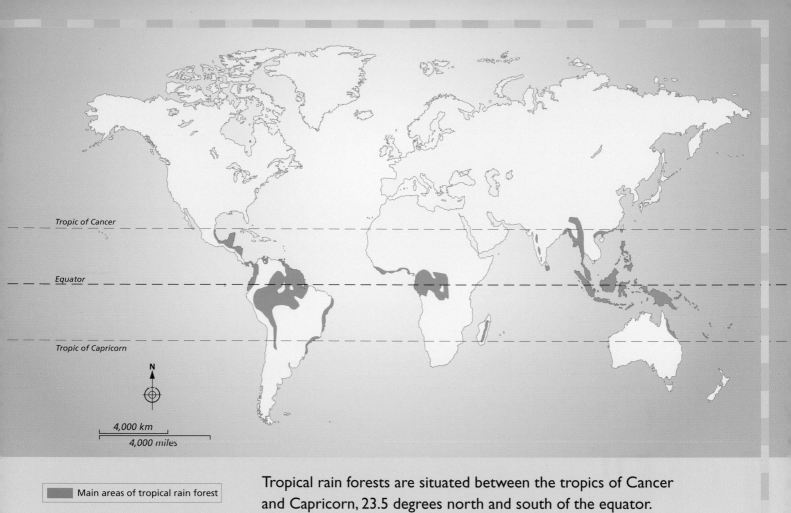

Tropic of Cancer

Equator

Tropic of Capricorn

N

4,000 km
4,000 miles

■ Main areas of tropical rain forest

Tropical rain forests are situated between the tropics of Cancer and Capricorn, 23.5 degrees north and south of the equator.

Central Africa, Southeast Asia, and parts of Australia and surrounding islands.

Temperate Rain Forests

Temperate rain forests are situated in Earth's temperate zones—between the Tropic of Cancer and the Arctic zone in the northern hemisphere and between the Tropic of Capricorn and the Antarctic zone in the southern hemisphere. Rarer than tropical rain forests, the temperate rain forests are mostly located near the sea. These rain forests are in western North America, Japan, Chile, Argentina, Taiwan, Australia, New Zealand, and some parts of east Asia.

Rain forests are among the oldest and richest habitats on the planet. They are home to more than half of all Earth's living species, but they are also some of the planet's most threatened environments. This book focuses on the issues facing tropical rain forests.

What Lives There?

Rain forests are home to an enormous variety of species. Perhaps 40 million different animal and plant species live there. In just 2.5 square miles (6.4 sq km) of tropical rain forest, there may be 750 tree species, 1,500 different kinds of flowering plants, 400 bird species, 150 types of butterflies, 125 different mammals, and 60 varieties of amphibians!

Many of the plants that grow in the rain forest may have uses as medicines. Less than 1 percent of tropical plants have been tested for medicinal purposes. Even so, one in four ingredients in Western medicines can be traced back to the rain forest. For example, the rosy periwinkle, which is found in the rain forests of Madagascar, is effective in the treatment of leukemia.

Despite the potentially useful medicines and the enormous biodiversity of the rain forests, huge amounts of the rain forest are destroyed each year. Approximately 57,915 square miles (150,000 sq km) of tropical rain forest are cut down and burned every year. This destruction releases more carbon dioxide (a gas that is linked to climate change—refer to page 11) into the atmosphere than all the cars, trucks, buses, and planes on the planet put together!

Who Lives There?

Up to 500 million people depend on the tropical rain forest for their homes, food, and livelihoods. Among these are 60 million indigenous people—the tribes who have lived in the forests for centuries, following a traditional way of life. These tribes include the Kayapo and Yanomami of the Amazon.

Through the generations, they have passed on a deep knowledge of medicinal plants, hunting, and growing and collecting food from the forests without causing permanent damage. This has allowed them to coexist in harmony with the other creatures and plants of the rain forest.

Today, increasing numbers of settlers are moving into the rain forests—people with no interest in living in harmony with the forest. Some are poor farmers who move into the rain forest because no one owns the land. They clear the trees so they can grow crops to feed themselves and their families. Rain forests are also being cleared on an industrial scale to make way for huge farms, mines, logging operations, and even hydroelectric power plants (see page 21).

A Baka tribesman from Cameroon snares a duiker. Rain forest peoples never take more than they need from the forest.

Rain Forest Products

Many of the goods we get from rain forests are obtained by causing damage or destruction. For example, many rain forest trees are felled for timber—an industry worth $16 billion a year. Palm oil is grown in plantations that have been created by destroying the rain forests in Indonesia and Malaysia. Palm oil is used in 10 percent of the items sold at the supermarket, including cookies, cakes, and even lipstick and floor polish!

Cattle ranching also destroys the rain forest. Brazil, which contains most of the Amazon rain forest, is now the world's biggest exporter of beef.

Planetary Climate Control

Rain forests regulate temperature and weather far beyond the forests. They help bring about regular rainfall, preventing floods and droughts. Every day, vast amounts of water evaporate from the forest floor and from the leaves of the trees in the tropical heat. The water vapor rises and condenses into clouds high above the forest. It then falls as rain later in the afternoon as the temperature decreases. The daily cycle of evaporation and rainfall means that the forest is neither too dry nor wet enough to cause flooding. The clouds that form over the rain forests often travel far beyond the forests, giving many countries the fresh water they need for drinking and growing crops.

Important for the planet, rain forests also retain huge amounts of carbon. The trees and plants take carbon dioxide from the air and water from the ground. Combined with sunlight, this creates the simple sugars they need to live and grow. This process is called photosynthesis. The rain forests create oxygen—which we need to breathe—as a by-product of photosynthesis. The plants of the rain forest retain far more carbon than plants living in any other land-based habitat—woodland, meadow, or plains, for example.

When the rain forests are cleared, they are normally burned. This means that all of the carbon they stored is released back into

This map shows how rain forests are among the most heavily exploited forests on the planet. Only the forests of North America and South Australia are being depleted more quickly.

the atmosphere as carbon dioxide. Carbon dioxide occurs naturally in the atmosphere and helps to trap the sun's heat that is reflected off the planet's surface. Called the greenhouse effect, it is similar to the way glass traps heat in a greenhouse. For this reason, carbon dioxide is known as a greenhouse gas. The more carbon dioxide there is in the atmosphere, the more heat is trapped, and the warmer the planet becomes—at least in some places. So the destruction of the rain forests is a major contributor to global climate change.

This book discusses issues that threaten rain forests across the globe. It focuses on particular regions to give examples of each of the issues—but many, if not all, of the issues are common to tropical rain forests everywhere.

Farming in the Amazon Rain Forest

The Amazon rain forest makes up 45 percent of the world's remaining tropical rain forest, covering almost 2 million square miles (5.2 million sq km). It spreads across Brazil, Bolivia, Peru, Colombia, Ecuador, Venezuela, Guyana, Suriname, and French Guiana. Brazil is the richest and most densely populated of the countries covered by the Amazon; it also has the highest rate of deforestation.

Since 1970, 232,000 square miles (600,000 sq km) of the Amazon rain forest have been lost. Between 2000 and 2006, nearly 58,000 square miles (150,000 sq km) of the forest were destroyed—an area larger than Greece. Why has Brazil lost so much rain forest in such a short time?

Shifting Cultivation

About one-third of the more recent loss of forest is due to shifting cultivators. These are poor farmers who move into the forest to grow crops. Often, they have moved there after being forced from their land by big corporations that set up large-scale operations in areas of the forest—perhaps a new cattle ranch, soy plantation, or a mine. In Brazil, many poor people are given areas of forest to cultivate by the government to help make them self-sufficient.

Shifting cultivators clear patches of rain forest for themselves, mostly by cutting down the trees and burning them—a process known as slash and burn. Many use the roads that have been carved through the forest by logging or mining

CASE STUDY

KAYAPO CULTIVATORS

Shifting cultivation, as practiced by indigenous peoples, used to be sustainable. The Kayapo Indians of Brazil clear an area by cutting down trees and setting a fire. They build houses from the wood and foliage. Further trees are cut down to extend the clearing and feed their fires. The ash provides nutrients for the soil. Women plant manioc, yams, beans, and pumpkins. After four or five harvests, the Kayapo move on. In the past, they would not have returned to that land until it had recovered its fertility (about 50 years later). Now, pressures from plantations and ranches mean that they often have to return much sooner and before the rain forest soil has recovered.

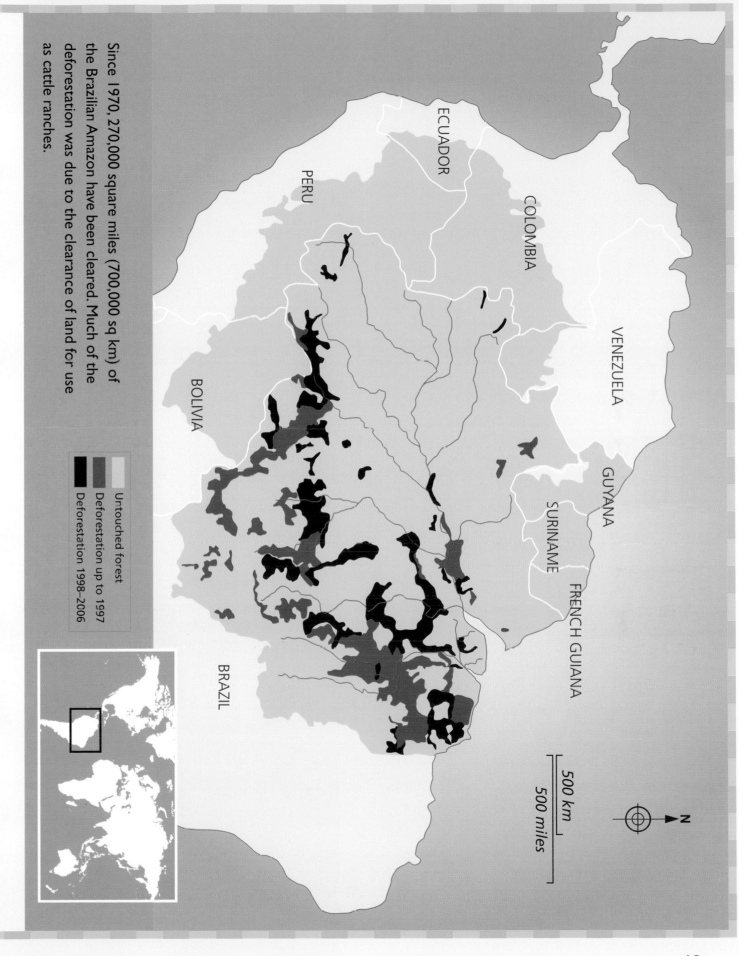

Since 1970, 270,000 square miles (700,000 sq km) of the Brazilian Amazon have been cleared. Much of the deforestation was due to the clearance of land for use as cattle ranches.

Untouched forest
Deforestation up to 1997
Deforestation 1998–2006

ECUADOR
PERU
COLOMBIA
VENEZUELA
GUYANA
SURINAME
FRENCH GUIANA
BOLIVIA
BRAZIL

500 km
500 miles

N

companies to gain access to areas of land deep in the forest. They clear the land to grow crops such as bananas, palms, rice, maize, or manioc.

Rain forest soil is very thin and lacking in nutrients. The forests appear fertile because dead leaves and animals are constantly being recycled. As the dead matter rots into the forest floor, it enriches the soil, allowing the forest to grow. When the trees are cleared to make way for crops, the supply of nutrients disappears with them. As a result, the soil becomes less fertile, so the farmers clear new areas.

Individually, these farmers do not use up much land—each one clears at least 2.5 acres (1 ha) per year—but with an estimated 500,000 farmers at work in the Brazilian Amazon, the impact of their activities soon adds up. Tens of thousands of small forest fires are observable by satellite every year.

Forests Make Way for Cows

The bulk of the farming-related deforestation is not, however, caused by shifting cultivators. According to estimates by Greenpeace, up to 80 percent of the destruction is caused by a few wealthy farmers who create enormous ranches for their cattle to graze on.

Cattle herders continue to turn more rain forest land into pasture for their herds. Much of the forest is not owned by anyone. According to Brazilian law, if someone clears an area of the forest, puts a few cattle on the land, and leaves them there for a year, that person is deemed to own the land.

The destruction of the rain forest to create pasture for cattle causes problems. While 2.5 acres (1 ha) of cleared land may be productive enough to support one cow for a year or two, the thin, poor rain forest soil is quickly eroded without tree roots to hold it together. After about seven years,

one cow may need to graze as much as 15 acres (6 ha) to survive for a year.

What's the Beef with Beef?

Solutions to the problems caused by cattle ranching are still a long way off. Brazil has global dominance in the beef market and plans to expand its herds. Producing more beef means the destruction of more rain forest. Furthermore, the expansion of

CATTLE RANCHING

Cattle ranching is now the biggest cause of deforestation in the Amazon. Nearly 80 percent of deforested areas in Brazil are used for pasture.

Greenpeace, January 2009

The blackened trunks of trees are reminders that this pasture in Brazil was, until recently, lush Amazon rain forest.

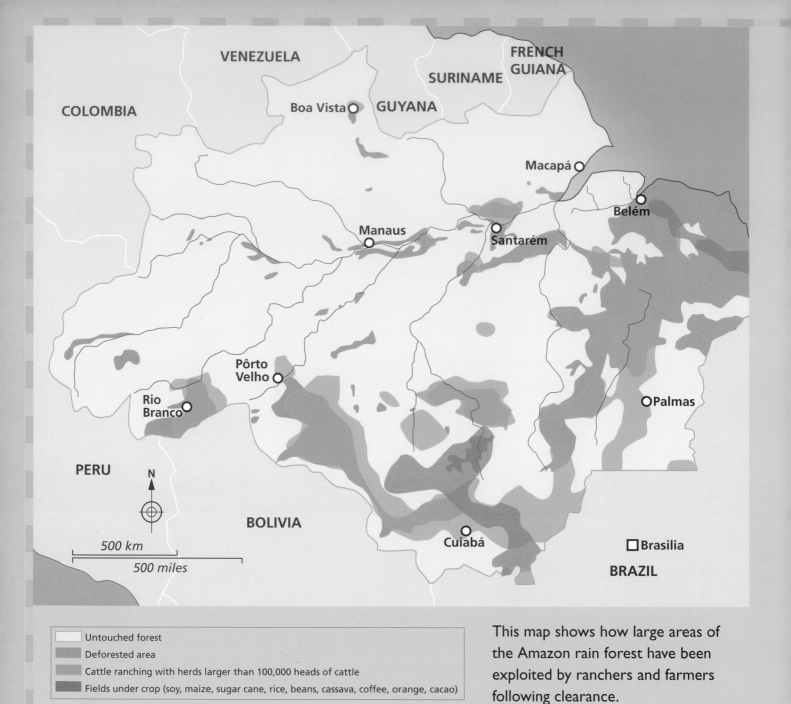

	Untouched forest
	Deforested area
	Cattle ranching with herds larger than 100,000 heads of cattle
	Fields under crop (soy, maize, sugar cane, rice, beans, cassava, coffee, orange, cacao)

This map shows how large areas of the Amazon rain forest have been exploited by ranchers and farmers following clearance.

cattle farming has an impact on the wider environment. Cows emit methane, which is a greenhouse gas. It is a greater contributor to global warming than carbon dioxide, though it is present in the atmosphere in much smaller quantities.

One way to discourage the expansion of cattle farming would be for governments to impose a climate tax on beef producers. Another option would be for Western governments to pay cattle ranchers to avoid destroying more of the rain forest.

As consumers, we can help by eating only locally produced beef.

Soy Fuels the Destruction

After cattle ranching, the biggest cause of rain forest destruction in the Amazon is soy bean plantations. Brazil is currently the world's second biggest exporter of soy beans after the United States. Soy is used as an ingredient in many foods for humans, but, more significantly, it is a major ingredient in animal feed.

Small farmers clear areas of forest, not to use themselves but to sell to large soy-growing companies. Rising demand has increased land values dramatically, further encouraging deforestation. In 1994, 2.5 acres (1 ha) of farmland in the soy-growing state of Mato Grosso, Brazil, was worth about $100. In 2010, that same land was worth more than $1,600.

Government Action on Soy

In 2006, Brazil imposed a moratorium (temporary prohibition) on soy plantations in newly deforested areas. Since then, less than 1 percent of newly deforested areas have been planted with soy. In 2008, the Brazilian government committed to reducing deforestation in the Amazon from 4,440 square miles (11,500 sq km) the previous year to 3,670 square miles (9,500 sq km).

However, not all farmers observe these restrictions. Approximately 10 percent of Brazilian soy is produced on illegal farms that use newly deforested land. The farmers disregard the law stating that 80 percent of a farm's land should be given over to the rain forest and only 20 percent of the land can be farmed. Nevertheless, the new law has drastically reduced the amount of land being cleared for growing soy beans, and soy is no longer seen as a major threat to the Brazilian Amazon.

CASE STUDY

PROTESTS IN SANTAREM

In 2002, a U.S. company, Cargill, built two grain silos, a $20 million terminal, and a port in Santarém, in the Brazilian state of Pará. In the following two years, deforestation around the port increased from 37,000 acres (15,000 ha) to 69,000 acres (28,000 ha). Land values rocketed and soy production soared as farmers rushed to take advantage of guaranteed sales. A local priest, Father Edilberto Sena, organized protests against the plant, saying: "If you fly over Santarém you can see what a desert it has become, you can see the damage of the pesticides and the lonely Brazil nut trees. Cargill has brought devastation to us; this is why we are fighting them."

Roads, Dams, and Climate Change

Many of the roads that carve their way through the Amazon rain forest have been built by industries to provide access for mines, logging operations, or agribusinesses. Once a paved road has been constructed, unofficial spur roads soon spring up in fishbone patterns, cutting deeper into the forest. These smaller roads open up new areas of previously untouched land to small farmers. They clear this land and grow crops on it for a few years. When the soil degrades, farmers turn it over to cattle grazing and clear yet more forest for crops.

Road to Ruin

The BR-163 is a Brazilian highway that runs 1,094 miles (1,760 km) between Cuiabá in the soy-growing Mato Grosso to Santarém. Much of the route remains unpaved. It costs about $80 to transport 1 ton (1 t) of soy from the Mato Grosso region to Atlantic ports such as Santarém. However, there are plans to finish paving the road. If this happens, it would cut the transportation cost to just $50 per 1 ton (1 t), delivering huge savings to the soy-growing agribusinesses in Mato Grosso. It is anticipated that up to 11 million tons (10 million t) of soy per year could eventually travel the BR-163, creating annual transportation savings of up to $320 million!

PERSPECTIVES

DANGEROUS DRIVE

Driving along the BR-163 is like taking part in a surreal rural video game. First, you must dodge waves of potholes that home in expertly on your vehicle. Next, ease your way past lumbering grain lorries whose tyres are prone to sudden explosions. As you pass fields of corn and soy, watch out for wandering cattle and the cowboys chasing them. And throughout, beware of kamikaze farm trucks rushing headlong towards you on the wrong side of the road.

Steve Kingstone, BBC News, September 26, 2006

This is an attractive idea to the agribusinesses of Mato Grosso and to their customers in Europe and China. However, the environmental costs of road building in the forest are huge. The Belém–Brasilia highway, completed in the 1970s, has now developed into an area of rain forest

Roads like this one in Brazil could soon cross the Amazon. These roads will give access to areas of forest that were previously unreachable.

A truck with a fresh load of soy beans at a soy storage warehouse in Mato Grosso, Brazil. The road-building program will make Brazil's soy industry more profitable.

A new road being built through the Amazon. Roads can have a disastrous effect on rain forest wildlife, disrupting the natural migration of animals.

destruction 250 miles (400 km) wide. A 2008 survey by the Carnegie Institution reported that 75 percent of rain forest destruction in Peru occurred within 12 miles (19 km) of a road. In Brazil, 95 percent of deforestation occurs within 31 miles (50 km) of a road.

Holding up the Roads

Multinational companies are attracted by the savings that could be made by building roads through the rain forest. For example, Honda, a Japanese company, ships approximately 1 million motorcycles to southern Brazil each year at a cost of

$42 per bike. The completion of the BR-163 highway could reduce this cost to $29 per bike, saving $12.5 million per year.

If Brazil is to continue its economic development, it needs good road links. This should be possible to achieve without too much cost to the environment, as long as it is not accompanied by the building of unofficial spur roads. If the government could enforce a freeze on unofficial road building, as well as ban the exploitation of forests surrounding the roads, Brazil could continue to grow its economy without fatally damaging its forests.

Dams: Cleaner, Greener Energy?

In Brazil, several tributaries of the Amazon River have been used for the creation of hydroelectric power (HEP). This is a means of generating electricity using flowing water. It involves the construction of huge dams across rivers, which lead to the creation of enormous lakes. The water from the lakes is periodically released through the dams via turbines, which spin as the water flows through them. The turbines create electricity as a result of their spinning action.

In one sense, HEP is a good form of energy. It does not produce any carbon dioxide in the creation of electricity. Damming rivers creates huge lakes, but this need not be a problem, and in dry parts of the world, it can even be a benefit. However, in species-rich areas such as the Amazon,

This area of rain forest was flooded as part of the Tucurui Dam project. Hydroelectric power generation has had a major impact on the Amazon.

CASE STUDY

TUCURUI DAM

The Tucurui Dam on the Tocantins River in Brazil was completed in 1984. By 2006, an estimated 40 million people received electricity generated by the dam. It produces 8,370 megawatts of electricity per hour. However, its construction flooded 940 square miles (2,430 sq km) of forest and forced 4,300 families to leave their homes. The dam had a serious impact on fisheries further down the river, causing the loss of many livelihoods. On the positive side, the area around the dam became much more prosperous as new businesses moved in, boosting employment.

flooding immense areas of rain forest displaces or destroys many animals and plants. The problem even extends to people. In many cases, tribes have been forced to leave homelands they have lived in for centuries to make way for the new lakes.

The Belo Monte Project

In 2010, the Brazilian government approved the construction of a new HEP project, Belo Monte, in the state of Pará. This was a bitter blow for environmentalists who had campaigned against it for 20 years. It will cost about $17 billion to build this project. It will involve damming parts of the Xingu River to create approximately 11,000 megawatts of electricity per hour—enough to power 23 million homes. However, the project will flood approximately 193 square miles (500 sq km) of rain forest. And that might not be the end of the story.

Between June and August, the river flow is weak, and power generation at this time of year is unreliable. To address this issue, the Brazilian government has proposed building another massive dam at Altamira, which would flood a further 2,355 square miles (6,100 sq km) of rain forest. Construction began on the dam in March 2011, but there continue to be protests and concerns over the environmental impact of the project.

PERSPECTIVES

BATTLES OVER BELO MONTE

We want to make sure that Belo Monte does not destroy the ecosystems and the biodiversity that we have taken care of for millennia. We are opposed to dams on the Xingu and will fight to protect our river.

Megaron Tuxucumarrae, Kayapo Indian chief, February 2010

There is not going to be an environmental disaster. Not a single Indian will be displaced. They will be indirectly affected, but they will not have to leave indigenous lands.

Carlos Minc, Brazilian Environment Minister, February 2010

Alternatives to HEP

In many ways, HEP is the obvious solution to energy production in the Amazon. With populations growing and energy needs increasing, Brazil and its neighbors need to increase their energy production capacity. HEP produces no greenhouse gases and is a clean, renewable energy source. However, HEP requires the flooding of valleys, which destroys hundreds, or even thousands, of acres of rain forest, threatening the many and diverse species of animals and plants that live there.

Each alternative has disadvantages. Conventional gas- or coal-fired power stations, though reliable sources of energy, produce huge quantities of carbon dioxide.

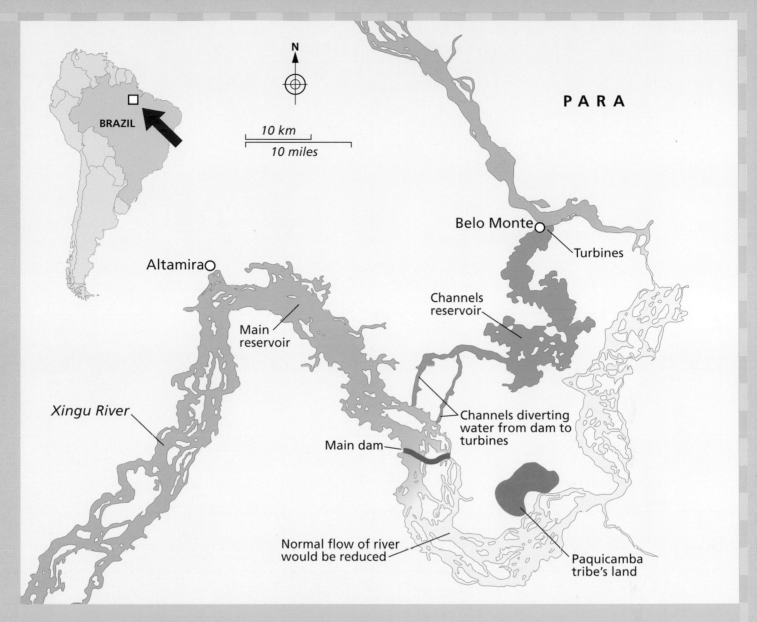

N

10 km
10 miles

PARA

BRAZIL

Altamira○

Belo Monte○
Turbines

Channels
reservoir

Main
reservoir

Channels diverting
water from dam to
turbines

Xingu River

Main dam

Normal flow of river
would be reduced

Paquicamba
tribe's land

The proposed Belo Monte dam project will largely divert the flow of the Xingu River into a newly formed reservoir. This will seriously affect the Paquicamba tribe, living near the river's present course, as the amount of water available to them will be drastically reduced.

Nuclear power does not produce any carbon emissions, but spent nuclear fuel remains deadly to humans for thousands of years and requires careful storage. Renewable energy sources, such as solar panels and wind turbines, involve similar levels of forest destruction to HEP, and, at the moment, they are too expensive. In the future, as technology advances and renewable energy generation becomes more affordable, it may be possible for the inhabitants of the forest to produce their own energy through microgeneration. In other words, they may use solar panels and wind turbines

Across the world, 2.5 acres (1 ha) of rain forest is lost every second. Tragically, very little recovers and regrows.

to provide the energy they need. Large-scale solar and wind energy generation is unlikely to be a reality in the Amazon.

The World's Problem

Apart from the habitat destruction caused by deforestation, there are other reasons why we should be concerned about the clearance of large areas of rain forest. Stored within the world's rain forests are an estimated 672 billion tons (610 billion t) of carbon. When trees are burned or cut down and left to rot, the carbon stored within them is released into the atmosphere. This contributes to global carbon dioxide emissions and, therefore, to climate change. More carbon dioxide is produced in one day of rain forest destruction than is caused by more than 8 million people flying from London to New York.

Carbon Stores

Destroying the rain forests not only releases carbon dioxide into the atmosphere, it also reduces the rain forests' capacity to absorb this gas. Through photosynthesis, rain forests absorb an estimated 5.3 billion tons (4.8 billion t) of carbon dioxide from the atmosphere each year, which is equivalent to 15 percent of human carbon dioxide emissions. Rain forest destruction is a major contributor to global warming. When the rain forest disappears, so does the cloud cover, which gives protection from the sun's heat and helps to lower ground temperatures by up to 9°F (5°C).

We Want to Develop, Too!

For all these reasons, many people in the developed world believe that, for the sake of the planet, it would be a good idea to encourage countries to preserve their rain forests.

However, these countries argue that the developed countries achieved their economic and industrial power at the expense of their own forests, most of which were cleared centuries ago. Rain forested countries contend that they also should be allowed to develop, which means converting parts of their rain forest into more productive, wealth-producing land. They want to be allowed to clear forested areas for timber or to grow crops or graze cattle.

If developed countries want this to stop, rain forested countries want compensation. But getting the world's governments to agree on how much to pay will be a huge challenge.

FACTS and FIGURES

CARBON DIOXIDE EMISSIONS

The Intergovernmental Panel on Climate Change (IPCC) estimates that 7.7 billion to 8.8 billion tons (7 to 8 billion t) of carbon dioxide are released into the atmosphere every year through the destruction of the rain forests. Up to 96 percent of these emissions are thought to originate from tropical rain forests. The rest comes from temperate rain forests. In total, it amounts to about 25 percent of all human-made carbon dioxide emissions, which is greater than the carbon dioxide produced by either the United States or China in a year.

Rain Forests of Southeast Asia

Southeast Asia is made up of a chain of 20,000 islands that covers 1.1 million square miles (2.9 million sq km). The rain forests of Southeast Asia are the oldest on the planet, dating back 70 million years. They are home to more species of plants and animals than the Amazon or African rain forests. Some experts fear that the forests of Southeast Asia could be destroyed by 2020. This chapter focuses on the issues affecting the rain forests of Indonesia and Papua New Guinea.

Indonesia

Indonesia in Southeast Asia is made up of 17,000 islands. It has almost 218.7 million acres (88.5 million ha) of forested land—55 percent of its total land area—and is the world's third largest rain forested zone after the Amazon and the Congo Basin. These forests are some of the most threatened. By 2005, in the space of just 15 years, 69 million acres (28 million ha) of forest were lost. The causes are varied, but most of it is due to logging or large-scale agriculture.

Indonesia's rain forests are home to 3,305 animal species and at least 29,375 plant species. More than 30 percent of the animals and almost 60 percent of the plants are found only in Indonesia. Almost one in ten of its animal species is threatened with extinction as increasing amounts of forest habitat is destroyed.

Logging in Indonesia

Indonesia is the world's largest exporter of tropical timber with a trade of $5 billlion a year. Logging permits have been issued for more than half of the

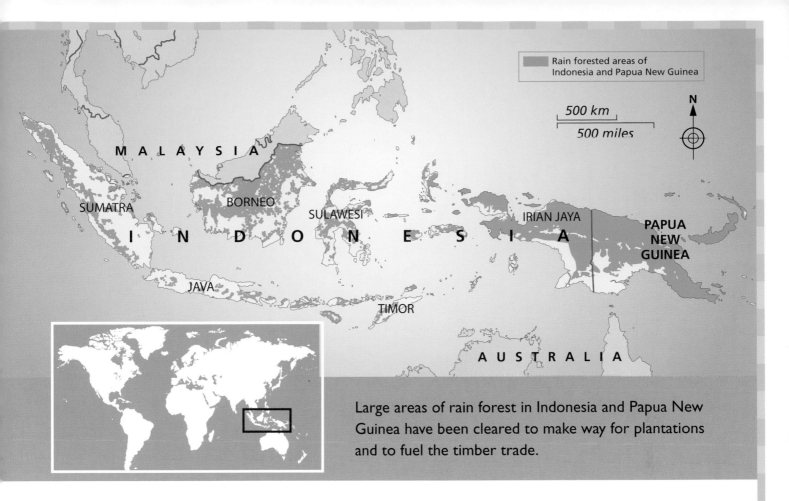

500 km

500 miles

N

MALAYSIA

SUMATRA

BORNEO

SULAWESI

IRIAN JAYA

PAPUA NEW GUINEA

INDONESIA

JAVA

TIMOR

AUSTRALIA

Large areas of rain forest in Indonesia and Papua New Guinea have been cleared to make way for plantations and to fuel the timber trade.

country's remaining forests of 118 million acres (48 million ha). The timber industry has gradually opened up some of the last great wildernesses on the planet. Areas that once were almost inaccessible are now in reach of the loggers, who constantly move deeper into the forests.

The destruction is occurring at an alarming rate. Since the mid-1990s, the number of logging grants in the remote Irian Jaya region has almost tripled and now makes up 20 percent of all concessions in Indonesia. Authorized loggers clear 1.7 million to 2.1 million acres (700,000 to 850,000 ha) of Indonesian rain forest each year. But the Indonesian government claims that up to 75 percent of the logging is illegal. Up to 6.9 million acres (2.8 million ha) of rain forest are destroyed annually when illegal logging is taken into account.

Despite a ban on their export, raw logs are smuggled to neighboring countries such as Malaysia and Singapore. Some officials accept bribes in return for ignoring illegal logging operations.

Papua New Guinea

Papua New Guinea (PNG) shares a large island with the Indonesian state of Irian Jaya. Between 1972 and 2002, PNG experienced the world's third largest forest losses (after Brazil and Indonesia) with a decline from 94 million acres (38 million ha) to 82 million acres (33 million ha).

LOGGERS IN PAPUA, INDONESIA

More than a quarter of the forests in Papua, Indonesia, have been sold off to logging companies.... [T]hese concessions last between 20 and 30 years. If the Indonesian government does nothing to stop logging concessions, soon all of our forests will be gone.

Christian Poerba,
Executive Director of Forest Watch Indonesia.

The University of Papua New Guinea and the Australian National University released a study in 2008 that estimated more than half of PNG's trees could be lost by 2021. The main causes are logging and large-scale palm oil plantations. When the loggers finish their work, farmers move in to finish clearing the land and then use it for agriculture.

The forest loss has been very rapid and on a scale similar to that of the Amazon. Current estimates suggest that PNG may lose more than half of its remaining rain forest by 2021. This is especially disturbing because PNG's rain forests contain more than 6 percent of the world's land species. They are also home to a surprising human cultural diversity, as 830 languages are spoken there—more than 10 percent of all languages spoken on Earth. Many of these are languages of the tribes living in the country's rain forests. If their way of life is lost, the chances are that their languages will die out also.

PNG has been struggling with a rapidly increasing population and has one of the highest rates of population growth in the world. With more than 6 million people to feed, more and more forested land is being cleared to make way for crops. This is understandable. But if the rest of the world wishes to save PNG's rain forests, another way to feed the country's people must be found.

The traditional way of life of forest peoples, like these tribesmen from Papua New Guinea, is under threat. If they die out, their cultures and languages will too.

Palm Oil in Indonesia

Since 2002, more land has been cleared to make way for oil-palm plantations. Palm oil is an inexpensive vegetable oil found in many of the products we consume. It is also used to create biodiesel, a fuel made from plants. As supplies could be used up within the next 20 to 30 years, growing our fuel may be a good solution to the coming energy crisis.

Between 2005 and 2010, demand for palm oil tripled in the United States. It also may become increasingly important in Europe. The European Union's Directive on the Promotion of the Use of Biofuels and Other Renewable Fuels for Transport (2003) requires that 5.75 percent of all fuel sold in Europe must be biofuel by December 31, 2010. This must increase to 13 percent by 2020. Most diesel now contains about 5 percent palm oil.

Biofuels come with a substantial cost to the environment. To make space for palm oil plantations, large areas of rain forest are slashed and burned. This releases huge amounts of carbon dioxide into the atmosphere. It has been estimated that it would take a palm oil plantation up to 840 years to soak up the carbon released by burning the forest to make way for it.

Each year in Indonesia, enormous areas of forest are set on fire before the monsoon season to make space for palm oil plantations. If the monsoon rains are delayed, fires can burn unchecked. This occurred in Indonesia in 1997–1998, when nearly 5 million acres (2 million ha) of forest were destroyed. Satellite analysis of the fires showed that 80 percent were linked to plantations or logging concessions. Burning is the fastest way to clear land for new plantations, but logged areas are also more likely to burn than untouched rain forest. After logging, debris is left on the ground, which can fuel fires. Without the shading effect of the canopy, the forest floor dries out, making fires more likely.

Palm Oil in Papua New Guinea

Palm oil plantations are springing up at an alarming rate in PNG. Vast areas of virgin forest are being swept aside to make way for the endless rows of palm trees. Local people band together to try and stop the plantations. They have seen what has happened elsewhere and are determined to protect PNG's forests. However, the multinational companies responsible for the rain forest clearances have huge economic power. In PNG, 97 percent of the land is community-owned. In order to establish their plantations, big companies obtain long-term leases that strip people of control. One of the methods companies use is to enter into partnerships with communities. The companies charge the communities for setting up new plantations and take 90 percent of the profits. The

CASE STUDY

KALIMANTAN

In the Indonesian territory of Kalimantan on the island of Borneo, a 4.9 million acre (2 million ha) palm plantation is planned. This has caused concern to environmentalists. Potentially, there are still many unknown plant and animal species in Borneo—361 new species were discovered there between 1994 and 2004.

A plantation worker harvests palm fruits in Indonesia's South Sulawesi province. Indonesia was the world's top producer of palm oil in 2009, producing 23 million tons (20.9 million t).

community has to continue to plant oil palms until their debts are paid.

Solutions for Southeast Asia
People power has some effect in PNG, but it will take more than that to ensure a safe future for its forests. In Indonesia, the situation is even more troubled. As long as officials are prepared to turn a blind eye to large-scale illegal logging, it is hard to envision how its rain forests can be protected.

Is REDD the Answer?
One possible solution to the problem would be for the rest of the world to pay rain forested countries to preserve their forests. This idea was proposed by PNG and nine other rain forest nations in 2005. They called it "reducing emissions from deforestation and forest degradation," or REDD. PNG argues that as the whole world benefits from the rain forests' survival, the whole world should pay toward their protection.

It is estimated that in 2007, up to 80 million tons (73 million t) of carbon dioxide were released through the burning of PNG's rain forests. If the world paid PNG $5 for each ton of carbon dioxide saved, this would amount to $365 million for the year. This far exceeds the official figure for the amount earned—$189 million—from timber exports from PNG for that year. Therefore, it would act as a tremendous incentive for the PNG government to protect its rain forests.

The idea appears to make sense. However, the countries of the world struggle to agree on how to value a ton of carbon dioxide. International climate change conferences, such as those in Bali in 2007 and Copenhagen in 2009, failed to reach agreement on this issue. Meanwhile, the forests continue to burn.

Sustainable Biofuel Certification
In June 2010, the European Union proposed a new voluntary code to certify biofuels for sustainability, ensuring that they are not sourced from oil-palm plantations that have been created by destroying rain forest. This is a step in the right direction, but the code needs to be international. If not, palm oil traders will simply sell their wares to other parts of the world with less stringent controls.

PERSPECTIVES

A PAPER AGREEMENT

This isn't anything more than a paper agreement if the financing isn't there to back it up.

Becky Chacko, Director of Climate Policy, Conservation International, speaking about REDD at the 2009 Copenhagen Climate Change Conference

Nature Reserves

Another way to protect the rain forests is to set up nature reserves. In September 2004, the Indonesian government responded to pressure from European and Japanese environmental groups by creating an ecosystem restoration concession—a 250,000 acre (101,000 ha) nature reserve of lowland rain forest in Sumatra, Indonesia. The reserve, known as the Harapan Forest, is home to 267 bird species, 66 of which are at risk of extinction, as well as endangered mammals, such as the Sumatran tiger, Asian elephant, and clouded leopard.

Orangutans are endangered in Borneo because of habitat destruction. There may be no more than 69,000 of them left.

Rain Forests of the Congo Basin

The Congo Basin in Africa is the world's second largest area of rain forest. It covers parts of Cameroon, the Central African Republic, the Democratic Republic of Congo (DRC), the Republic of Congo, Equatorial Guinea, and Gabon. More than 75 million people depend on the forests for their existence. The forests are also home to some of Africa's best known wild animals, including chimpanzees, gorillas, and forest elephants.

Taxation and Corruption

In recent years, the forests of the Congo Basin have been badly damaged by commercial logging and destruction for subsistence agriculture (small-scale agriculture by farmers for themselves and their families only), both of which have been caused, indirectly at least, by civil war. Logging has increased significantly since peace returned to the region as countries desperately try to generate new wealth.

The governments in the Congo Basin impose taxes on the logging companies. Officially, the revenue raised from these taxes is to pay for the provision of health care, education, and other essential services for the poor people of the region. Instead, much of it ends up in the pockets of corrupt officials. In many areas, the enforcement officers, who are supposed to prevent illegal logging operations, are ill-equipped to do

FACTS and FIGURES

LOGGING IN THE DRC

There has been a moratorium on logging in place since 2002, but despite this, more than 37 million acres (15 million ha) of the DRC's forest have been sold to the logging industry. That's an area five times the size of Belgium.

Source: Greenpeace

their jobs. Often, they have only bicycles to patrol huge areas of rain forest.

The indigenous people of the forests are offered items by the logging companies, such as bags of salt or crates of beer, in return for the destruction of the places where they live. The logging companies promise them hospitals, schools, and proper sanitation, but the people are left with nothing. Often, they are simply forced to move to new areas as the forest they depend on for food and shelter is destroyed around them.

Roads Open Up the Forests

A network of roads is expanding in the Congo Basin rain forest. Researchers have studied satellite photographs of the 4 million square miles (10.4 million sq km) of Congo Basin rain forest, taken between 1976 and 2003, and found 32,000 miles (52,000 km) of logging roads.

As elsewhere in rain forested areas, the roads provide access to areas of forest that were previously difficult or impossible to reach. Once the loggers have moved on, the small farmers can move into an area, burn off the remaining forest, and plant crops.

During the 1990s and early 2000s, civil war in the DRC drove many people from their homes. The roads gave these refugees access to new land, enabling them to clear forest and grow food.

Pygmy Tribes

The Congo is the world's second largest river by volume after the Amazon. Its rain forests comprise about 70 percent of Africa's plant cover. The forests teem

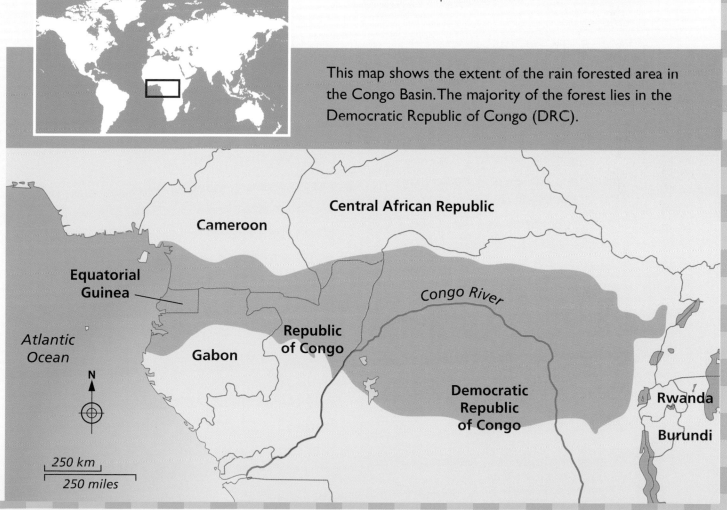

This map shows the extent of the rain forested area in the Congo Basin. The majority of the forest lies in the Democratic Republic of Congo (DRC).

with life with more than 600 tree species and 10,000 animal species. The forests are also inhabited by Pygmy tribes, including the Mbuti of northern DRC; the Twa of eastern DRC, Rwanda, and Burundi; the Baka of southern Cameroon; and the Aka of the Central African Republic and northern Congo. In total, approximately 150,000 forest peoples are spread over a huge area, averaging less than one person for every 1.5 square miles (4 sq km).

Pygmies are small in stature. Even the tallest of the tribes, the Mbuti, rarely grow taller than 5 feet (1.5 m). Being small has proved an advantage in the dense forests and makes moving about through the trees much easier. Smaller body area also allows Pygmies to dissipate body heat better—an advantage in the hot and steamy conditions of the rain forest.

Pygmies live in small groups of up to 70 people. They move several times a year to different parts of the forest to find food supplies, carrying all that they own on their backs. Their nomadic way of life has little impact on the rain forest, because they never overexploit any one area.

When tribes set up a new settlement, they clear away the undergrowth and small trees. They leave the canopy to provide shelter from the sun and rain. They live in houses that look like igloos, but these are made from saplings and leaves woven together to form a shelter.

Pygmy Poachers

Pygmies are excellent hunters, but traditionally, they never took more game than they needed and had a great respect for their prey. Now, these forest peoples are increasingly being hired as trackers by poachers (illegal hunters of protected animals) who are trying to find forest elephants. Pygmies are also hunting for more and more "bushmeat" (the meat of wild African animals) to trade with the villagers who fled to the rain forests during the recent civil wars.

CASE STUDY

LOGGERS AND PYGMIES

Logging is a massive threat to the Pygmies' way of life by destroying the forests the Pygmies need to survive. Logging roads open up the forests, bringing new settlers from other areas. Some settlers carry diseases that the Pygmies have never encountered before and have no immunity against. The loggers bring new items to trade, including tobacco, marijuana, and alcohol—substances that many Pygmies have become addicted to. Loggers also bring a new idea with them—money. This encourages the Pygmies to exploit their forests in a way they never have before. There is a real danger that without protection, the forest people's way of life will be lost forever.

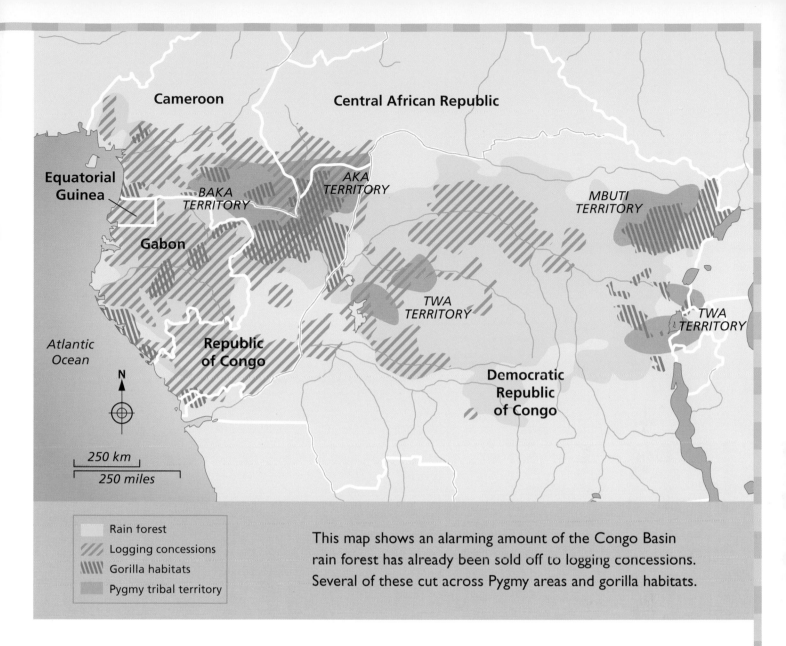

This map shows an alarming amount of the Congo Basin rain forest has already been sold off to logging concessions. Several of these cut across Pygmy areas and gorilla habitats.

Legend:
- Rain forest
- Logging concessions
- Gorilla habitats
- Pygmy tribal territory

250 km
250 miles

Refugees in the Rain Forest

The civil war in the DRC has forced huge numbers of its people to relocate. As many as 375,000 people are thought to have taken shelter within the boundaries of the country's Virunga National Park, which is home to more than half of the world's remaining population of mountain gorillas.

These people need wood to burn for their cooking fires, to build their houses, and to make tools. The park's area of pristine rain forest is shrinking because of the trees the newcomers are cutting down. Aid agencies and the United Nations supply these people with sufficient wood to meet their needs, so they do not have to cut down more of the forest, but this cannot be a long-term solution. Instead, the settlers are being trained to look after the protected areas and are being shown how preserving their forests for the future can encourage tourism in the region. Tourists, who come from

These refugees of the civil war in the DRC have been forced to seek refuge in the rain forest after their homes were attacked by soldiers.

much wealthier countries in the West, spend money during their visits. Much of this money will find its way to the local people.

The Wild Meat Trade

With so many very poor people living in the rain forest, it's not surprising that some turn to poaching to feed themselves. Unfortunately, they are targeting endangered mountain gorillas and forest

MASTER MAPPERS

People in the Congo Basin rarely own the land they live on even if they have been there for many years. There is nothing to stop governments from selling the land to loggers. A charity, Rain Forest Foundation UK, has trained Congolese Master Mappers to travel into the remote Inongo territory in western DRC and work with nearly 100 rain forest villages. The Master Mappers are teaching 660 villagers to use GPS devices (instruments that use satellite signals to determine location) to produce detailed maps that will prove their existence to loggers and to the DRC government. Hopefully, this will prevent more logging concessions in the area.

as tourist areas. They are also training people to help preserve protected areas. In many areas, the government has imposed bans on wild meat trading. In Cameroon, villagers are being trained to use trenches and fencing around their small farms to stop elephants from ruining their crops.

Increasingly, the elephants are being monitored by agencies such as the World

elephants. If this situation continues, some of these spectacular large mammals could face extinction. A similar story is unfolding across the Congo Basin, where elephants are being hunted in the forests of Cameroon for their ivory tusks. They are also being killed to prevent them from damaging farms. If a herd of elephants raids a small farm, a farmer's entire annual harvest can be ruined.

Solutions

Conservation charities and aid agencies work with forest communities to show them how valuable their forests could be

Gorillas reproduce quite slowly—at about the quarter of the rate of most mammals. The targeting of gorillas by hunters has had a disastrous effect on the number of gorillas.

Wildlife Fund (WWF) by using electronic tags. This helps to detect incidents of poaching and enables researchers to learn more about elephant behavior. WWF and other environmental groups use their global influence to try to ban trade in ivory. If successful, this will remove any incentive for poaching.

Mining

The Congo Basin is rich in mineral deposits. These include iron, copper, manganese, uranium, gold, and diamonds. This fact has not escaped the attention of international mining companies. Some have managed to secure very lucrative deals. New mining operations cause deforestation and water pollution. Roads and railways that provide the means to get the minerals from mines to markets open up previously inaccessible areas of forest for bushmeat hunting and poaching.

The Belinga Project

In July 2007, the government of Gabon agreed to a deal with CMEC, a Chinese mining company, to create an iron ore mine in the Gabonese rain forest. The Belinga Project, as it was known, would cover 3,000 square miles (7,700 sq km) of land. It would also include the construction of a hydroelectric dam near Kongou Falls. The mining road would be carved 1,160 square miles (3,000 sq km) through Ivindo National Park, which is a conservation area. It is home to chimpanzees, western lowland gorillas, buffalo, and forest elephants.

The Gabonese government failed to carry out a proper assessment of the environmental impact of this project. It also did not consult properly with the local people about how the project would affect them. The mine, once built, would destroy entire ecosystems. The damming of the Ivindo River would flood villages and drive numerous animal species from their homes. By giving the go-ahead for the project, the government broke its own code on national parks. The code states that the national parks were established to preserve "the wealth of the ecosystem . . . for current and future generations" and to encourage "the development of ecotourism as an economic alternative to the exploitation of natural resources."

The Brainforest group, led by prize-winning environmentalist Marc Ona Essangui, helped the affected communities organize protests against the mine and dam project. The Gabonese government met with the protesters and agreed to look at the project again. In May 2008, the deal was renegotiated on terms that were more sensitive to environmental concerns. The project was scaled down to 232 square miles (600 sq km), and there would be no road building through the national park.

PERSPECTIVES

FLOODED LAND, POLLUTED WATERS

All the villages upstream of the dam will be flooded and people displaced. People drink the water of the river and fish in it; they'll lose their livelihoods. Near the mine, the water will be polluted.

Gabonese environmental activist
Marc Ona Essangui

Mines like this gold mine in the DRC bring people deep into the rain forest in search of their fortunes. Deforestation and pollution tend to be the results of such operations, many of which are poorly regulated.

The Future of the Forests

The world's rain forests are home to millions of people and vast numbers of animal and plant species. Almost certainly, thousands of species are still to be discovered—many of which may hold cures to diseases. Furthermore, the rain forests play a crucial role in maintaining Earth's climate and acting as a check against global warming. We destroy them at our peril.

A Global Challenge

Humans are becoming aware that rain forests make a massive contribution to the world's climate, and we destroy them at our peril. Billions of tons of carbon dioxide are locked away in the forests. By destroying the forests, we release more greenhouse gases into the atmosphere. This is the most likely reason why the planet's rain forests will be preserved. The developed world understands that rain forests have much more value to the planet as they are than they do as timber, paper, beans, or oil.

It is essential that we protect these amazing environments for the future, not just to save the people, animals, and plants that live there, but to ensure that we prevent climate change from spiraling out of control. Hopefully, with education, humanity will agree in time to value the rain forests as they are.

How You Can Help

The problems facing the rain forests are massive. It's easy to wonder what kind of difference one person could make. Even though your influence as an individual may be small, many individuals acting together can make a difference. Action could include supporting organizations that campaign for rain forests and influencing those around you, such as your family members, in what they do and buy.

Use Consumer Power

Next time you shop, look for a Fair Trade logo or a Rainforest Alliance logo on the foods you buy. These labels indicate that the farmers who grew the crop received a fair payment for it and had good working and living conditions. The logo indicates the crop was grown on a farm committed to protecting the environment.

SAVE THE FORESTS

If we do nothing else, save the rain forest ... most biologists believe that the rapid destruction of the tropical rain forests and the irretrievable loss of the living species dying along with them, represent the single most serious damage to nature now occurring.

Earth in the Balance: Forging a New Common Purpose by Al Gore (Earthscan Publications, 2007)

A cause for hope: in this part of the Amazon rain forest, palm tree seedlings have been planted to help the forest regenerate itself.

Avoid Palm Oil

Look at the ingredients of the products in the supermarket. If an item contains palm oil, and it does not indicate that the palms have been sustainably grown, avoid it. Sustainably grown palms have not had a negative effect on the rain forests.

Ethical Wood

When buying products, such as furniture or paper, made from tropical wood, look for the FSC (Forest Stewardship Council) mark. This indicates that the wood has come from managed forests.

Help a Rain Forest

Through some organizations, you can "adopt" 1 acre (0.4 ha) of rain forest in return for a donation. Donations are used to buy new land, to plant trees, and to pay staff to look after the forest and prevent poaching.

Glossary

agribusiness A large-scale farming enterprise.

biodiversity The range and variety of species to be found within a given habitat.

biofuel A fuel produced from dry organic matter or combustible oils produced by plants.

canopy The top layer of trees, which act like a roof for the rain forest.

climate change Long-term, significant change in Earth's climate, usually seen as resulting from human activity.

conservation Preservation of the natural environment.

deforestation The clearing and destruction of forested areas.

developed countries The wealthiest nations in the world, including Western Europe, the United States, Canada, Japan, Australia, and New Zealand.

ecosystem A community of living things plus the physical environment they depend on.

endangered species A species whose numbers are so small that the species is at risk of extinction.

erode Rocks and other deposits on Earth's surface are gradually worn away by the action of water, ice, wind, and other natural agents.

European Union (EU) An economic and political association of European countries.

exploitation Using something for selfish or unethical reasons.

global warming An increase in Earth's temperature. Global warming has occurred in the distant past as the result of Earth's natural cycles. Today, the term is used to refer to the warming linked to human activity.

greenhouse gases Gases that trap the sun's heat in the atmosphere.

habitat The environment in which an animal or plant normally lives or grows.

humidity The amount of water vapor in the atmosphere.

hydroelectric power (HEP) Electric power generated by using flowing water to drive a turbine that powers a generator.

indigenous Originating in and characteristic of a particular region or country.

multinational company A business that operates in more than one country.

nature reserve An area of land that is managed in order to preserve its wildlife, vegetation, and physical features.

nutrients Substances that provide essential nourishment for plants and animals.

photosynthesis The process by which plants convert sunlight, water, and carbon dioxide into food, oxygen, and water. The plants "breathe in" carbon dioxide and "breathe out" oxygen.

plantation A large estate on which crops are raised, often by resident workers.

shifting cultivation A farming system in which farmers move from one place to another when the land becomes exhausted.

subsistence agriculture A type of farming in which all the produce is consumed by the farming family.

sustainable Conserving the environment by avoiding depletion of natural resources.

temperate Characterized by moderate temperatures.

Further Information

Books

Essential Habitats: Tropical Rain Forest Habitats by Barbara Taylor (Gareth Stevens Publishing, 2007)

Global Questions: Why Are the Rainforests Being Destroyed? by Peter Littlewood (Arcturus Publishing, 2011)

Horrible Geography: Bloomin' Rainforests by Anita Ganeri (Scholastic, 2008)

Planet Earth: Rain Forests by Steve Parker (QEB Publishing, 2008)

Web Sites

www.greenpeace.org/usa/en/campaigns/forests/forests-worldwide/congo-rainforest/
This Green Peace site discusses how the rain forests in the Congo are being destroyed.

www.rainforest-alliance.org/kids
This Rainforest Alliance site includes a Frequently Asked Questions section.

www.rainforestfoundation.org/
The Rainforest Foundation site provides a section on indigenous people and the protection of rain forests. It also includes a Commonly Asked Questions and Facts section, as well as 10 things you can do to save the rain forests.

www.savetherainforest.org
This site discusses rain forest plant life, rain forest animals, causes of rain forest destruction, and facts about the rain forests.

Index

Page numbers in **bold** refer to maps and photos.